P9-CER-852

To: Mom

From:
Ruth

The Spirit of Christmas
A History of Best-Loved Carols

By Virginia Reynolds

Designed by Lesley Ehlers

 PETER PAUPER PRESS, INC.
WHITE PLAINS, NEW YORK

For Dad, who loves a song and a story

Special thanks to Sally Hupp and
Michael Domis for their help and guidance

See page 57 for information on the paintings that
appear throughout this book.

Images copyright © 2000
Art Resource
Text copyright © 2000
Peter Pauper Press, Inc.
202 Mamaroneck Avenue
White Plains, NY 10601
All rights reserved
ISBN 0-88088-414-2
Printed in China

7 6

Visit us at www.peterpauper.com

Contents

And, lo, the angel of the Lord came upon them, and the glory of the Lord shone round about them; and they were sore afraid.

And the angel said unto them, Fear not: for, behold, I bring you good tidings of great joy, which shall be to all people.

For unto you is born this day in the city of David a Saviour, which is Christ the Lord. And this shall be a sign unto you; Ye shall find the babe wrapped in swaddling clothes, lying in a manger.

And suddenly there was with the angel a multitude of the heavenly host praising God, and saying,

Glory to God in the highest,
and on earth peace,
good will toward men.

LUKE 2:9-14 KJV

Introduction

———◆———

*W*hat would Christmas be without our beloved Christmas carols? We sing them while we're decking our halls, dancing with the sugarplums, and hanging our stockings by the chimney with care. We sing carols with our loved ones, and teach them to our children.

Christmas carols and music have been with us since the earliest days. People began singing songs of praise at Christmas as far back as the 5th century—not long after the early Christian church created the holy day of Christmas.

Many of our favorite carols were written during the Middle Ages. Ballads told poetic stories with musical accompaniment. Minstrels carried these "musical stories" from town to town, singing joyfully about the Holy Family and the Nativity.

Most of the carols we sing originated in European countries, and reflect their wonderfully distinct traditions. Some carols were written by great composers, others by devout clergymen. People sang them both in humble churches and in magnificent cathedrals, just as they do today.

There are fascinating stories behind all of our favorite Christmas carols, stories that we retell in *The Spirit of Christmas*. These stories will enrich your celebration as you sing your best-loved carols, and listen to them on the enclosed CD. Music revives the wonder and joy we feel every year as Christmas draws near. Music embodies the Spirit of Christmas.

V. R.

O Come, O Come, Emmanuel

---◆---

WORDS AND MUSIC: TRADITIONAL, 9TH CENTURY
TRANSLATION: JOHN MASON NEALE, 1851

Therefore the Lord himself shall give you a sign;
Behold, a virgin shall conceive, and bear a son,
and shall call his name Immanu-el.

ISAIAH 7:14 KJV

The roots of this hymn are quite ancient, dating back to some of the earliest known liturgies—somewhere around the 9th century. Originally, this song was a "plainsong," or Gregorian chant, and monks sang it *a cappella* (without instrumental accompaniment). During medieval times, chants were a primary form of musical expression, and an important part of all religious services. Monks sang a special series of chants during the Christmas period. This chant, known as the *Magnificat*, was sung between December 17 and December 23, in honor of the upcoming Nativity. On each night, a different monk was chosen to sing that day's portion of the chant, which took place at the canonical hour of *vespers*. The refrain that we sing today was added later.

The English clergyman John Mason Neale translated the hymn into English in 1851. Active in Church affairs, Neale pursued a lifelong interest in church architecture and, despite poor health, worked extensively among the needy. He translated and adapted more than 400 hymns, including *Good King Wenceslas* (which is not a Christmas carol at all, but a song pertaining to St. Stephen's Day, December 26).

O Come, O Come, Emmanuel

O come, O come, Emmanuel,
And ransom captive Israel,
That mourns in lonely exile here
Until the Son of God appear.

Rejoice! Rejoice! Emmanuel
Shall come to thee, O Israel!

O Come, Thou Rod of Jesse, free
Thine own from Satan's tyranny.
From depths of Hell Thy people save,
And give them vict'ry o'er the grave.

Rejoice! Rejoice! Emmanuel
Shall come to thee, O Israel!

O come, Thou Day-spring come and cheer
Our spirits by Thine advent here,
And drive away the shades of night,
And pierce the clouds and bring us light.

Rejoice! Rejoice! Emmanuel
Shall come to thee, O Israel!

O come, thou Key of David,
And open wide our heavenly home;
Make safe the way that leads on high,
And close the path to misery.

Rejoice! Rejoice! Emmanuel
Shall come to thee, O Israel!

God Rest Ye Merry, Gentlemen

The first line means "Gentlemen, may God keep you in good spirits"—a blessing.

Immensely popular throughout its history, this carol even merits a mention by Charles Dickens in his famous tale, *A Christmas Carol.* It's also a very old carol, and was almost certainly sung by wandering groups of singers called *waits.* In "Merrie Olde England," music was an important part of everyday life. Minstrels carried the news of the day from town to town and were often handsomely rewarded for their efforts. In many towns, the *waits* played the role of "town criers," singing the hours of the day and reporting local happenings. Christmastime kept them especially busy. As they strolled through the snowy streets, they told the story of the Nativity in song, adding to the festive atmosphere. Townspeople would show their appreciation by giving the singers money or food.

Another familiar song that the *waits* sang is *We Wish You a Merry Christmas.* After imparting their good wishes, the *waits* singers felt entitled to ask for some "figgy pudding"!

God Rest Ye Merry, Gentlemen

God rest ye merry, gentlemen; let nothing you dismay.
Remember, Christ our Savior was born on Christmas Day
To save us all from Satan's pow'r, when we were gone astray.

O tidings of comfort and joy, comfort and joy!
O tidings of comfort and joy!

In Bethlehem, in Israel, this blessed Babe was born,
And laid within a manger upon this blessed morn;
The which His Mother Mary did nothing take in scorn.

O tidings of comfort and joy, comfort and joy!
O tidings of comfort and joy!

From God our heav'nly Father, a blessed angel came;
And unto certain shepherds brought tidings of the same;
How that in Bethlehem was born the Son of God by name.

O tidings of comfort and joy, comfort and joy!
O tidings of comfort and joy!

Good Christian Men, Rejoice

WORDS: HEINRICH SUSO, 14TH CENTURY
TRANSLATION: JOHN MASON NEALE, 1853
MUSIC: GERMAN, 14TH CENTURY

Angels visited the Dominican monk Heinrich Suso in a dream one night, singing and dancing joyfully. Suso joined them in their dance, and wrote down this carol immediately upon waking. The original words are partly in Latin and partly in German. This type of song writing that mixes languages was called a *macaronic*. An example is:

In dulci jubilo
Nun singet und seid froh.

(In sweet jubilation, let us our homage show.)

Four hundred years later, in 1745, worshipers at the Moravian Mission in Bethlehem, Pennsylvania sang this carol in 13 languages including Dutch, Latin, Greek, and Mohawk!

Many musicians have revised the carol, including Johann Bach, who wrote a very complex arrangement. Although there are several English translations, the one we usually use today was written by John Mason Neale.

Good Christian Men, Rejoice

Good Christian men, rejoice
With heart and soul and voice.
Give ye heed to what we say;
News! News!
Jesus Christ is born today.
Ox and ass before Him bow,
And He is in the manger now.
Christ is born today!
Christ is born today!

Good Christian men, rejoice
With heart and soul and voice.
Now ye hear of endless bliss:
Joy! Joy!
Jesus Christ was born for this!
He hath open'd the heav'nly door,
And man is blessed evermore.
Christ was born for this;
Christ was born for this.

Good Christian men, rejoice
With heart and soul and voice.
Now ye need not fear the grave:
Peace! Peace!
Jesus Christ was born to save.
Calls you one and calls you all
To gain His everlasting hall.
Christ was born to save;
Christ was born to save.

Joy to the World

---◆---

WORDS: ISAAC WATTS, 1719
MUSIC: LOWELL MASON, CA. 1848

The words of this carol are based on Psalm 98, which reads:

> *Make a joyful noise unto the LORD, all the earth:*
> *make a loud noise, and rejoice, and sing praise. . . .*
> *make a joyful noise before the LORD, the King.*
> PSALMS 98:4-6 KJV

In 1719, the English minister Isaac Watts published a collection of hymns entitled *The Psalms of David, Imitated in the Language of the New Testament.* Watts was a prolific composer, and wrote more than 600 hymns for children and adults, many of which are still sung today. Among his many admirers was Benjamin Franklin, who published the first American edition of *The Psalms of David* in 1729.

The origin of the music, which was written over a century later, is more difficult to trace. For many years, people thought that Handel wrote the music. A little bit of musical detective work earlier this century revealed that the music's composer was actually Lowell Mason, "the father of American church music." Mason was the first music teacher in an American public school and co-founder of the Boston Academy of Music. He devoted his life to music education, eventually composing more than 1,600 religious works. A humble man, Mason greatly admired Handel, and eventually served as president of Boston's Handel and Haydn Society. Perhaps this explains why people erroneously attributed this tune to Handel. Mason called his composition *Antioch*, a reference to the Syrian city where Jesus' disciples first came to be called "Christians."

Joy to the World

Joy to the world! The Lord has come:
Let earth receive her King.
Let ev'ry heart prepare Him room,
And heav'n and nature sing, and heav'n and nature sing,
And heav'n, and heav'n and nature sing.

Joy to the world! The Savior reigns:
Let men their songs employ,
While fields and floods, rocks, hills and plains
Repeat the sounding joy, repeat the sounding joy,
Repeat, repeat the sounding joy.

He rules the world with truth and grace,
And makes the nations prove
The glories of His righteousness
And wonders of His love, and wonders of His love,
and wonders, wonders of His love.

Hark! The Herald Angels Sing!

—◆—

WORDS: CHARLES WESLEY, 1739
MUSIC: FELIX MENDELSSOHN, 1840

Felix Mendelssohn once commented that this music, which he wrote to commemorate Johann Gutenberg and the invention of the printing press, would not be suitable for a hymn or church music. How wrong he turned out to be!

Formerly, the words to this hymn were: *"Hark, how all the welkin [heaven] rings! Glory to the King of Kings!"* The hymn's composer, Charles Wesley, didn't originally intend this as a Christmas hymn, but perhaps as a hymn for Easter. Wesley, co-founder of the Methodist Church, wrote more than 4,000 hymns over the course of his life. George Whitefield, Wesley's friend, later added the first two lines as we now sing them.

An organist named W. H. Cummings decided to adapt Mendelssohn's music to Wesley's hymn. He arranged the 10-line stanzas that we sing today, and published the carol in 1856.

Hark! The Herald Angels Sing!

Hark! The herald angels sing,
"Glory to the newborn King!
Peace on earth and mercy mild,
God and sinners reconciled."
Joyful, all ye nations rise,
Join the triumph of the skies;
With the angelic host proclaim,
"Christ is born in Bethlehem!"

Hark, the herald angels sing,
"Glory to the newborn King!"

Christ by highest heav'n adored;
Christ the everlasting Lord!
Late in time behold Him come,
Offspring of a Virgin's womb.
Veiled in flesh the Godhead see;
Hail the incarnate Deity.
Pleased as man with man to dwell,
Jesus, our Emmanuel!

Hark, the herald angels sing,
"Glory to the newborn King!"

Hail the heav'n-born Prince of
    Peace!
Hail the Son of Righteousness!
Light and life to all He brings,
Ris'n with healing in His wings.
Mild He lays His glory by,
Born that man no more may die.
Born to raise the sons of earth;
Born to give them second birth.

Hark, the herald angels sing,
"Glory to the newborn King!"

The Hallelujah Chorus
(from The Messiah)

WORDS AND MUSIC: GEORGE FRIDERIC HANDEL, 1741

*D*id you ever wonder why the audience always stands up during *The Hallelujah Chorus?* Apparently, at the first London performance of *Messiah* (1743) in the Covent Garden Theatre, King George II was in the audience, and rose to his feet as the choir began singing this chorus. When the King stood, everybody stood. However, just why King George stood up is a little unclear; he might have been stretching his legs, or he may have so admired the music that he stood up as a gesture of respect for Handel. Whatever the reason, this custom remains with us, and is a common tradition throughout the English-speaking world.

Initially, *The Messiah* was meant to be sung at Easter time, not Christmas. (The performance that King George allegedly attended took place in March.) This composition is known as an *oratorio*, an epic type of musical composition for full orchestra and many voices, and usually depicting a sacred story. *Messiah* was a personal favorite of its composer George Frideric Handel, who wrote it in just three weeks during 1741. First performed in Dublin the following spring, *The Messiah* is comprised of three sections representing Jesus' birth, death, and resurrection. Each section contains dramatic solo pieces and soaring choral passages.

Wolfgang Amadeus Mozart revised parts of *The Messiah* in 1788. He tried to reflect the musical tastes of the day, and to make the score less dependent upon the organ, which was not always available to accompany the singers. Mozart also re-wrote some of the choral parts. Although Mozart's revisions survive, many conductors and performers today prefer Handel's original music, in the interest of historical authenticity.

During the 19th century, the British performed *oratorios* with huge numbers of singers and musicians, both professional and amateur. At one 1834 performance, over 600 voices sang *The Messiah* at London's Crystal Palace before a crowd of 3,000. It was an extremely popular piece with all classes. Profits from ticket sales were donated to charity, which may have led to more performances of *The Messiah* at Christmas time.

The Messiah is a very long work, but most listeners are familiar with *The Hallelujah Chorus*. Although the lyrics are simple, the intricate harmonies, together with the magnificent score, combine to produce a powerful piece of choral music, with a magnificent crescendo of voices. When we listen to *The Hallelujah Chorus*, we can sense the "multitude of the heavenly host praising God."

The Hallelujah Chorus

Hallelujah! Hallelujah!
Hallelujah! Hallelujah! Hallelujah!

Hallelujah! Hallelujah!
Hallelujah! Hallelujah! Hallelujah!

For the Lord God Omnipotent
*   reigneth.*
Hallelujah! Hallelujah! Hallelujah!
Hallelujah!

The Kingdom of this world is become
The Kingdom of our Lord and of His
Christ, and of His Christ;
And He shall reign for ever and ever
And He shall reign for ever and ever

King of Kings,
For ever and ever. Hallelujah!

Hallelujah!
And Lord of Lords,
For ever and ever. Hallelujah!
Hallelujah!

King of Kings, and Lord of Lords,
And He shall reign for ever and ever
And He shall reign for ever and ever

King of Kings,
And Lord of Lords.
Hallelujah! Hallelujah! Hallelujah!
Hallelujah! Hallelujah!

O Come, All Ye Faithful

(Adeste Fideles)

———◄●►———

WORDS: JOHN FRANCIS WADE, 1740-44
TRANSLATION: FREDERICK OAKELEY, CA. 1840
MUSIC: JOHN READING

There's a great deal of myth and conjecture about this much-loved Christmas standard, which many English people still refer to as the "Portuguese Hymn." Until about 1900, people believed that this hymn could be traced as far back as the 13th century, and that St. Bonaventure possibly composed the original Latin words.

Alas, it's unlikely that either of these theories is true. A clergyman living in Buckfast Abbey named Dom John Stéphan, who was a musical detective of sorts, researched the original manuscript, and discovered that John Francis Wade wrote it. Wade, a Roman Catholic, lived in Douay, France, where he earned his living copying and teaching music. Composed between 1740 and 1744, the hymn became quite well known locally. In fact, a parody of the hymn appeared in a comic opera of the day!

Adeste Fideles became popular among Roman Catholics during the latter half of the 18th century, and traveled to England by way of the Portuguese Embassy, which performed the hymn regularly at its services.

Verses that further reconstructed the Gospel record of the Nativity were added during the early part of the 19th century, but later dropped by the translator, Frederick Oakeley.

Oakeley's English translation followed almost 100 years after the original words. Also a Roman Catholic clergyman, Oakeley was a Canon of Westminster Cathedral in London. The translation probably helped the carol become popular with non-Catholic singers. The carol is commonly sung today both in English and in Latin.

O Come, All Ye Faithful

O come, all ye faithful,
Joyful and triumphant,
O come ye, O come ye to Bethlehem.
Come and behold Him, born the
King of angels.

O come, let us adore Him,
O come, let us adore Him,
O come, let us adore Him,
Christ, the Lord.

Sing, choirs of angels,
Sing in exultation;
Sing all ye citizens of heav'n above:
Glory to God in the Highest.

O come, let us adore Him,
O come, let us adore Him,
O come, let us adore Him,
Christ, the Lord.

Yea, Lord, we greet Thee,
Born this happy morning;
Jesus, to Thee be glory giv'n;
Word of the Father, now in flesh
appearing.

O come, let us adore Him,
O come, let us adore Him,
O come, let us adore Him,
Christ, the Lord.

Adeste fideles,
Laeti triumphantes,
Venite, venite in Bethlehem.
Natum videte, Regem angelorum.
Venite adoremus;
Venite adoremus;
Venite adoremus, Dominum.

Silent Night

WORDS: JOSEPH MOHR, 1816
MUSIC: FRANZ GRUBER, 1818

Silent Night possesses a simple dignity and power, like the alpine setting where it was written. It has been translated into almost every language.

Popular legend states that Joseph Mohr, the carol's composer, a village priest in the little Austrian town of Oberndorf, penned the words to *Silent Night* on Christmas Eve. He became distraught when the organ in his church broke down and couldn't be repaired in time for Christmas services. He enlisted his friend, musician Franz Gruber, to compose a guitar accompaniment for his hymn. *Silent Night* was first performed at Midnight Mass in St. Nicholas' Church, not grandly with a somber organ accompaniment, but humbly, with a guitar and a few voices.

Silent Night was in fact first sung on Christmas Eve in 1818, although there really isn't any evidence to suggest a broken organ, or other crisis. We don't know why Joseph Mohr selected a guitar accompaniment for his

hymn, but the choice was fortunate. The image of the starry sky, the little church, and the lone guitar is one of enduring humility and quiet beauty. Mohr wrote several arrangements for *Silent Night*.

Word of the "Tyrolean Folk Song" (as it came to be called) spread throughout Europe. Traveling folk singers brought the carol to the royal courts, and even to America, where the Rainer Family performed it in 1839. For a time, the song's origins were confused, and many believed it the work of a great composer. An original manuscript by Mohr crediting Gruber with the melody was discovered in 1994, setting the record straight.

Mohr continued in his career as a parish priest until his death in 1848, and donated all his earnings to charity.

Silent Night

Silent night, holy night,
All is calm, all is bright.
Round yon Virgin Mother and Child,
Holy Infant so tender and mild,
Sleep in heavenly peace;
Sleep in heavenly peace.

Silent night, holy night,
Shepherds quake at the sight.
Glories stream from heaven afar,
Heav'nly hosts sing Alleluia;
Christ the Savior is born;
Christ the Savior is born.

Silent night, holy night,
Son of God, love's pure light.
Radiant beams from Thy holy face,
With the dawn of redeeming grace,
Jesus, Lord, at Thy birth;
Jesus, Lord, at Thy birth.

Ave Maria

——◆——

FRANZ SCHUBERT, 1825

Ave Maria (Hail Mary) is really a way of addressing the Virgin Mary, as the Angel Gabriel did when he foretold Jesus' birth:

> *Hail, thou that art highly favored, the Lord is with thee:*
> *blessed art thou among women.*
>
> LUKE 1:28 KJV

The angel's annunciation to Mary is an important part of the Christmas story, and Christians throughout history have highly revered the Virgin Mary. Christians repeat the angel's greeting every time they say the prayer *Hail Mary.*

Ave Maria has been set to music many times, but probably the most famous *Ave Maria* was written by Austrian composer Franz Schubert in 1825. However, it was intended as a piece of secular, not sacred music. During his short career, Schubert, using a Romantic style, wrote many German songs called *lieder.* Most of these songs are based on folk tales and literature of the time. Schubert composed the music of *Ave Maria* to accompany a portion of Walter Scott's *The Lady of the Lake.* The song, called *Ellen's Song III,* is a prayer to the Virgin Mary in German. The Latin translation is presented here.

Ave Maria

Ave Maria!
gratia plena,
Maria, gratia plena,
Maria, gratia plena,
Ave, Ave. Dominus,
Dominus tecum.
Benedicta tu in mulieribus,
et benedictus,
et benedictus fructus ventris,
ventris tui, Jesus.
Ave Maria!

Ave Maria!
Mater Dei,
Ora pro nobis peccatoribus,
Ora, ora pro nobis
Ora, ora pro nobis peccatoribus,
Nunc, et in hora mortis,
et in hora mortis nostrae,
et in hora mortis, mortis nostrae
et in hora mortis nostrae.
Ave Maria!

The First Noël

The old French word *Noël* comes from the Latin word *Natalis*, meaning "birth" or "birthday"—specifically the birth of Christ. *Natalis* is also the root for the word *Nativity*. Many European languages have developed similar words such as *Natal* (Spanish) and *Natale* (Italian). The original English spelling of the word was *Nowell*, but by the 14th century Chaucer (in *The Canterbury Tales)* used the modern spelling.

Although you might guess that *The First Noël* originated in France, we can't be sure of that. It may have accompanied a "Miracle Play" during the 13th or 14th century. These plays dramatized Bible stories and holy events for the public, and were very popular throughout Europe.

The first written record of this carol appeared in William Sandys' 1833 edition of *Christmas Carols, Ancient and Modern.* Sandys lived in London, but traveled to Devon and Cornwall in southwest England to collect the tunes in his book. He is responsible for rescuing many carols and folk songs from obscurity.

Folk songs enjoyed a revival in 19th century England, and there are several collections like Sandys' that include this carol. Some suspect that the carol originally contained additional verses but, if so, these have not survived.

Another interesting fact is that *The First Noël* refers to an event that is not recorded in the Bible: although we know that the three Wise Men saw the Star of Bethlehem, the Bible doesn't mention that the shepherds saw it. This carol is so popular, however, that modern singers are prepared to forgive the historical inaccuracy.

The First Noël

The first Noël, the angel did say,
Was to certain poor shepherds in fields as
   they lay;
In fields where they lay keeping their
   sheep,
On a cold winter's night that was so deep.

Noël, Noël, Noël, Noël,
Born is the King of Israel.

They looked up and saw a star,
Shining in the East beyond them far;
And to the earth it gave great light,
And so it continued day and night.

Noël, Noël, Noël, Noël,
Born is the King of Israel.

This star drew nigh to the northwest;
O'er Bethlehem it took its rest,
And there it did both stop and stay,
Right o'er the place where Jesus lay.

Noël, Noël, Noël, Noël,
Born is the King of Israel.

O Holy Night

WORDS: PLACIDE CAPPEAU DE ROQUEMAURE, 1847
MUSIC: ADOLPHE-CHARLES ADAM, CA. 1847
TRANSLATION: JOHN SULLIVAN DWIGHT

A French bishop described *O Holy Night* soon after its publication as having a "lack of musical taste and total absence of the spirit of religion." Fortunately, people didn't take his criticism to heart, and this carol has earned its place as a Christmas classic. The poetry and music infuse the beauty and magnificence of the first Christmas with new meaning.

Adolphe Charles Adam, who also composed the ballet *Giselle*, wrote the music for *O Holy Night*. Despite disapproval from the church, Adam enlisted the help of his friend, poet Cappeau de Roquemaure, who wrote the original words, entitled *Cantique de Noël*.

An American, John Sullivan Dwight, translated the carol into the words we sing today.

O Holy Night

O holy night, the stars are brightly shining;
It is the night of the dear Savior's birth.
Long lay the world in sin and error pining,
Till He appeared and the soul felt its worth.
A thrill of hope, the weary soul rejoices,
For yonder breaks a new and glorious morn.
Fall on your knees,
Oh, hear the angel voices!
O night divine, O night when Christ was born!
O night, O holy night, O night divine!

Led by the light of faith serenely beaming,
With glowing hearts by His cradle we stand.
So led by light of a star sweetly gleaming,
Here came the wise men from the Orient land.
The King of Kings lay in lowly manger,
In all our trials born to be our friend.
He knows our need,
To our weakness no stranger.
Behold your King! before the lowly bend!
Behold your King! your King! before Him bend!

Truly He taught us to love one another;
His law is love and His gospel is peace.
Chains shall He break, for the slave is our brother,
And in His name all oppression shall cease.
Sweet hymns of joy in grateful chorus rise we,
Let all within us praise His holy name.
Christ is the Lord,
Then ever, ever praise we;
His pow'r and glory ever more proclaim,
His pow'r and glory ever more proclaim.

It Came Upon the Midnight Clear

WORDS: EDMUND HAMILTON SEARS, 1849
MUSIC: RICHARD STORRS WILLIS, 1850

Edmund Hamilton Sears was a Unitarian minister and graduate of Harvard's Divinity School. His original writings came to the attention of Oliver Wendell Holmes, who praised him highly. Sears, who preferred a quiet life among his New England congregation, emphasized Jesus' message of "peace on earth, good will toward men." The message of "peace" rings throughout this carol, as it rang in the hills around Bethlehem on the first Christmas. The words to *It Came Upon the Midnight Clear* first appeared in print in 1850 in the *Christian Register*.

By contrast, composer Richard S. Willis led a very public life as an editor and critic with *The New York Tribune*. A student of Mendelssohn and a musical journalist, Willis composed carols while acting as a vestryman at The Little Church Around the Corner in New York City. The music of the carol we sing today was actually written for another carol, *While Shepherds Watched Their Flocks by Night*, and was matched with Sears' words several years later.

Although Sears and Willis were from similar backgrounds, they never met.

It Came Upon the Midnight Clear

It came upon the midnight clear
That glorious song of old,
From angels bending near the earth
To touch their harps of gold.
"Peace on the earth, goodwill to men,
From heav'n's all-gracious King."
The world in solemn stillness lay
To hear the angels sing.

Still through the cloven skies they
    come
With peaceful wings unfurl'd;
And still their heav'nly music floats
O'er all the weary world.
Above its sad and lowly plains,
They bend on hov'ring wing;
And ever o'er its Babel sounds
The blessed angels sing.

For lo! the days are hast'ning on,
By prophets seen of old,
When with the ever-circling years
Shall come the time foretold.
When the new heav'n and earth
    shall own
The Prince of Peace, their King,
And the whole of world send back
    the song
Which now the angels sing.

Angels We Have Heard on High

WORDS: TRADITIONAL FRENCH
TRANSLATION: JAMES CHADWICK, 1862
MUSIC: TRADITIONAL

An old myth suggests that the 2nd century Pope Telesphorus so loved a particular *Gloria* that he ordered it sung every Christmas Eve during midnight mass. The *Gloria* so beloved by the early Pope became the Latin refrain of the carol.

Although the story of Pope Telesphorus is very interesting, it's more likely that the music for *Angels We Have Heard on High* dates from the 18th century.

This carol contains two parts that were joined together during the 19th century. The verses are part of a French carol called *Les Anges dans nos Campagnes* (Angels in Our Fields), and the French have sung it for centuries. Just as the shepherds in the hills around Bethlehem sang songs of praise on the first Christmas, Provençal shepherds traditionally sang in their fields on Christmas Eve, trying to recreate the wonder of another, earlier group of shepherds—shepherds who witnessed something miraculous.

The *Gloria* is traditional, with no known composer. *Glorias* are brief, repetitive songs of praise, sometimes having very complex choral melodies, that have been sung at Christmas services for centuries. This *Gloria* conjures up an image of singing angels on a wintry night in Bethlehem, raising their voices in songs of praise.

Angels We Have Heard on High

Angels we have heard on high
Sweetly singing o'er the plains,
And the mountains in reply
Echoing their joyous strains.

Gloria in excelsis Deo,
Gloria in excelsis Deo.

Shepherds, why this jubilee?
Why your joyous strains prolong?
What the gladsome tidings be
Which inspire your heav'nly song?

Gloria in excelsis Deo,
Gloria in excelsis Deo.

Come to Bethlehem and see
Him whose birth the angels sing.
Come adore on bended knee
Christ the Lord, the newborn King.

Gloria in excelsis Deo,
Gloria in excelsis Deo.

What Child Is This?

WORDS: WILLIAM CHATTERTON DIX, 1865
MUSIC: TRADITIONAL ("GREENSLEEVES")

The melody *Greensleeves* is so old that it's impossible to date. There are dated references to *Greensleeves* as far back as 1580, and it may be that English King Henry VIII actually wrote it, but the melody probably predates his realm. We know that Good Queen Bess (Elizabeth I) danced to the melody and that Shakespeare mentions it in *The Merry Wives of Windsor*. It's had many different sets of lyrics, most of which weren't at all religious. One version describes the lament of a jilted lover. Others are downright bawdy.

As with many other carols, traditional music made a late marriage to sacred words. The English hymn writer William Dix composed these words under the title *The Manger Throne*. *Greensleeves* had, at last, become respectable.

What Child Is This?

What Child is this, who laid to rest,
On Mary's lap is sleeping?
Whom angels greet with anthems sweet
While shepherds watch are keeping?

Chorus
This, this is Christ the King,
Whom shepherds guard and angels sing.
Haste, haste to bring Him laud,
The Babe, the Son of Mary.

Why lies He in such mean estate
Where ox and ass are feeding?
Good Christian, fear for sinners here,
The silent Word is pleading.

Chorus
This, this is Christ the King,
Whom shepherds guard and angels sing.
Haste, haste to bring Him laud,
The Babe, the Son of Mary.

So bring Him incense, gold and myrrh;
Come, peasant king, to own Him.
The King of Kings salvation brings;
Let loving hearts enthrone Him.

Chorus
This, this is Christ the King,
Whom shepherds guard and angels sing.
Haste, haste to bring Him laud,
The Babe, the Son of Mary.

O Little Town of Bethlehem

WORDS: PHILLIPS BROOKS, 1868
MUSIC: LEWIS H. REDNER, 1868

As Phillips Brooks approached the village of Bethlehem on Christmas Eve, 1866, he imagined the Holy Family on their journey nearly two thousand years before, walking over the very same stones, toward the tiny town. Brooks was overcome by the beauty and peace of Bethlehem and his experience inspired him to write this song. He claimed that the Holy Land was "still singing in [his] soul" when he wrote *O Little Town of Bethlehem* for a children's Sunday school class two years later.

On Christmas Eve 1868, Brooks, rector of Holy Trinity Church in Philadelphia, asked the church organist to set his verses to music. The next morning, Lewis H. Redner brought the completed hymn to church, where the children's choir sang it for the first time.

O Little Town of Bethlehem

O little town of Bethlehem,
How still we see thee lie;
Above thy deep and dreamless sleep,
The silent stars go by.
Yet in thy dark streets shineth
The everlasting Light;
The hopes and fears of all the years
Are met in thee tonight.

For Christ is born of Mary,
And gather'd all above,
While mortals sleep, the angels keep
Their watch of wond'ring love.
O morning stars together
Proclaim the holy birth,
And praises sing to God the King
And peace to men on earth.

O holy child of Bethlehem,
Descend to us, we pray;
Cast out our sin and enter in;
Be born to us today.
We hear the Christmas angels,
The great glad tidings tell;
O come to us, abide with us,
Our Lord Emmanuel.

Away in a Manger

WORDS: ANONYMOUS LUTHERAN, CA. 1885
MUSIC: JAMES R. MURRAY, 1887

People still call this delightful song "Luther's Cradle Hymn," and believe that Martin Luther sang his own children to sleep with it in the 15th century. None other than the song's composer, James Murray, promoted this charming fable. We really don't know who wrote the words, only that they appeared anonymously in a Lutheran publication called *Little Children's Book for Schools and Family* in 1885.

When the music first appeared in a children's hymnal two years later, it was entitled "Luther's Cradle Hymn." James Murray, the editor of the hymnal, wrote that the song was "composed by Martin Luther for his children, and still sung by German mothers to their little ones." Murray, who was a student of Lowell Mason *(Joy to the World)*, then added his own initials to the end of the song, thereby ensuring over a century of confusion.

Away In a Manger

Away in a manger, no crib for a bed,
The little Lord Jesus laid down His sweet head.
The stars in the sky looked down where He lay,
The little Lord Jesus asleep on the hay.

The cattle are lowing, the poor Baby wakes,
But little Lord Jesus no crying He makes.
I love Thee, Lord Jesus, look down from the sky,
And stay by my cradle till morning is nigh.

Be near me, Lord Jesus, I ask Thee to stay
Close by me forever and love me I pray.
Bless all the dear children in Thy tender care,
And take us to heaven to live with Thee there.

ART CREDITS

p. 6: Melozzo da Forli (1438-1494), *Musical Angel with Viola.*
© Scala/Art Resource, NY

p. 13: Lorenzo d'Alessandro, *Musical Angels.*
© Alinari/SEAT/Art Resource, NY

p. 18: Memling, Hans (1425/40-1494), *Angels with Musical Instruments.*
© Scala/Art Resource, NY

p. 22: Lotto, Lorenzo (1480-1556), *Angel Gabriel, detail from Annunciation.*
© Alinari/SEAT/Art Resource, NY

p. 26: Angelico, Fra (1387-1455), *Dancing Angels, detail from Last Judgment.*
© Scala/Art Resource, NY

p. 31: Melozzo da Forli (1438-1494), *Angel Playing the Lute/Musical Angel
with Lute.* © Scala/Art Resource, NY

p. 36: Lippi, Fra Filippo (1406-1469), *Angels, detail from the Coronation
of the Virgin.* © Scala/Art Resource, NY

pp. 40-41: Baciccio (1639-1709), *Musical Angels.* © Scala/Art Resource, NY

p. 45: Melozzo da Forli (1438-1494), *Music-making angel (with lute).*
© Scala/Art Resource, NY

p. 50: Gentileschi, Artemisia, *Saint Cecilia.* © Scala/Art Resource, NY